World Religions General Editor: Raymond F. Trudgian

THINKING
ABOUT ISLAM

JOHN B. TAYLOR

Director, Dialogue with people of Living Faiths and Ideologies,
World Council of Churches

LUTTERWORTH EDUCATIONAL
GUILDFORD, SURREY

First published 1971

Revised edition 1983

Lutterworth Educational

For permission to reproduce the photographs the author and publishers are indebted to the Keystone Press Agency (for numbers 1, 2, 3, 5, 6, 7, 10, 12, 14, 15 and 16), to the Camera Press Agency (for numbers 4, 8, 9, 11 and 17) and to the Pakistan Embassy (for number 13).

The author is further indebted to Allen and Unwin for permission to quote from A. J. Arberry's translation of the Qur'an in *The Koran Interpreted* and to Oxford University Press for permission to quote from A. Guillaume's translation of Ibn Isḥāq in *The Life of Muhammad*.

The editor is grateful to Mawlana M.Z.A. Ansari of Karachi and Mr. Eric Rolls of Westhill College for critically reading the manuscript.

Conventional symbols have been used in writing Arabic proper names and technical terms in English script. An exception has been made in the case of familiar words such as Islam (Islām) and Muhammad (Muḥammad).

ISBN **0 7188 2583 7**

Printed in Great Britain by
Fletcher & Son Ltd, Norwich

CONTENTS

LIST OF ILLUSTRATIONS

EDITOR'S INTRODUCTION

The teaching of World Religions has taken a place in religious education in this country for some time. Often, however, it was left until the sixth form when a rapid survey of at least two or three religions per term was made, at the end of which pupils were expected to 'compare' these with Christianity. The most that could be hoped for in such a situation was an acquaintance with the historical founder of a particular faith and knowledge of the more unusual customs and traditions associated with its followers who were thought of as living in some other part of the world.

In recent years the situation has changed so dramatically that a new approach is called for. Not only are many of those faiths now represented in our schools, but mosques and temples form a communal focal point for new immigrants as the synagogues have done for immigrants of another era. Even in areas where the other faiths are not represented the situation presents searching questions through newspaper items and television documentaries.

Long before the sixth form therefore a majority of children will have some knowledge of other religions through their own community or the mass media. For an increasing number this knowledge begins in the primary school.

It follows that the school leaver and certainly the student teacher in a college of education will want to look more deeply at a religion other than their own. Ideally at this stage time should be given to one faith only or students could follow a thematic study through the beliefs of the main world religions. Themes such as the nature of God, the meaning of worship, the problem of evil and suffering, war and peace are but a few of the rewarding studies which could be carried out. In this way some approach can be made to another culture, another faith which will provide both understanding and enrichment in preparation for living in the plural society.

This series of 'Thinking about' books is presented with this need in

7

mind. Each deals with one faith only and the text has been prepared by a member of that faith or by Christians of deep sensitivity who have brought their awareness of the religious dimension and their academic training to a presentation of a sympathetic portrayal of another faith.

Not only do they deal with matters of theology and practice but also the social and political implications of each living faith are drawn out for the reader. It is true that we can never begin fully to understand another faith until we have lived for some time in the country where that faith is practised by the majority of people. It is hoped however that these books will begin the quest and be related to the search for truth in such disciplines as geography, as we try to understand why particular countries have adapted a certain faith, in history, as we see man searching for an identity often motivated by religion, and in social studies as we see how mankind has sought to live in meaningful communities.

Apart from its educational value this series is presented in the hope that it will play its part in enhancing community relations in this country. It is some time now since the Rt. Hon. Roy Jenkins (when he was Home Secretary) defined integration as 'not a flattening process to produce "carbon copies" of Englishmen, but equal opportunity accompanied by cultural diversity in an atmosphere of mutal tolerance'.

This book seeks to bring that tolerance to the cultural and religious diversity in our society in the hope that whatever the faith of the readers they will understand their own faith at a deeper level as through this book they come into contact with another world faith, and that through their study they will develop a deeper and wider conception of religion.

As a member of the Advisory Team of the Christian Education Movement with special responsibility for advising teachers and pupils on the study of World Religions I trust that this series will go some way to help the need which is daily expressed in our mail by teachers, student teachers and pupils alike.

RAYMOND F. TRUDGIAN
Annandale, 1971

1

THE ONE GOD

The Meaning of Islam

Islam is not only the name of a great religion. It is a word which describes a relationship between man and God. This relationship of submission (*islām* in Arabic) means that God is Lord of man, and man is the servant of God. The servant is dependent upon his Lord, and is obedient to him; and so the man who has accepted this submission, dependence and obedience is called 'submitted to God' (*muslim*).

These Arabic words, *islām* and *muslim*, are given an important place in the teaching of the Prophet Muhammad (570–632 A.D.). He and his followers devoted themselves as servants to the One God and were therefore called Muslims. Their religion and their way of life were called Islam.

It is useful to remember the way in which the words Islam and Muslim have a basic spiritual meaning behind them. It is also important to see that spiritual relationships are not only expressed in religious worship but also in a whole way of life. This book is about things which Muslims believe, but it is also a book about what Muslims have done and do because of what they believe. For Muslims religion is a way of life.

The Way to Become a Muslim

It is not necessary to undergo a special course of training and teaching to become a Muslim. Children who are born of Muslim parents are regarded as being Muslims. Others who desire to become Muslim need only say, sincerely and with true intention, the following confession of faith: 'I bear witness that there is no god but God, and that Muhammad is the Prophet of God'. These words are used throughout a Muslim's life:

1. Muslims praying in a London mosque

they are first recited aloud into the new-born infant's ear; they are learned in their Arabic form (*La ilah illa Allah*) while the Muslim child is still young; they are spoken with true intention when the child is coming to maturity; they then become a daily confirmation of his acceptance of Islam.

It will be noticed that in this book the word *Allah* is translated by God. If a Christian were speaking or writing Arabic he would use the word *Allah* to express Jehovah or God. The word *Allah* does not refer only to one god of a particular people, say the Arabs; it refers rather to the One God of all men, the Creator of all, the Supporter of all, the Judge of all. So it is best translated in English by the word God.

When the Muslim makes his confession that 'There is no god but God' he is rejecting the idea that man should offer his service and obedience to any imagined deity or to any idol. We shall see that Muhammad lived at a time when his fellow Arabians were bewildered and sometimes exploited by the claims of worshipping a whole series of divinities and spirits, many of which were honoured by idol cults, sacrifices and superstitious rituals. In place of these, Muhammad urged men and women to go back to the monotheistic faith in the One God.

Monotheism Before Islam

Muslims believe that God had sent many prophets to the various people of the world before the time of Muhammad, and that these had all summoned men to the true faith of Islam. In particular there had been the many Jewish prophets, among whom Muslims give pride of place to Abraham, Moses and David. Muslims also regard Jesus as a prophet of the One God. But Muslims believe that Jews and Christians distorted their scriptures. They also recall various other figures from early Arabian culture, and these too are regarded as prophets whose messages were neglected, distorted and despised. It was this past and persistent disobedience by men towards God's communication through his prophets that made so timely, in Muslim belief, the preaching of the Prophet Muhammad.

The Qur'an, which, as we shall see, is the holy book which Muhammad experienced as coming to him from God, speaks of men's neglected faith in the One God. The Qur'an asks men why they appeal to God when they are in an emergency like a storm at sea, or why they utter oaths in the name of God. It then asks why men who seem to recognize God's power in the most difficult situations go on to waste their energies in appealing to other false deities. (See Surah 10, verses 13 and 23).

We know from the Qur'an and also from some pre-Islamic poetry that there were certain men at the time of Muhammad who were called *hanīfs*. They too were reminding men that there was only One God and that they should restore the simple faith of Abraham whom they saw as father of all the Semitic peoples, Arabs, Jews, and Mesopotamians, and whose One God they saw as the Lord of all mankind. But the preaching of these *hanīfs* was of very limited appeal, and it was for the Prophet Muhammad to sweep away the old idolatry and to establish Islam as a universally preached and all-embracing creed of faith in One God.

Jews and Christians in Arabia

Some scholars have suggested that the monotheism which Muhammad preached was suggested to him by Jews and Christians. However these Jews and Christians, who had often escaped from persecution in neighbouring countries, used different languages, especially for their worship and their scriptures; there were no Arabic translations of the Old Testament or the New Testament until after Islam had become established. Furthermore the Jewish and Christian communities kept themselves aloof from the pagan Arabs and made little or no attempt to preach to them or to invite them to join their religious community.

Another reason why the Christians, in particular, were somewhat withdrawn was that many of them were involved in various internal arguments with fellow Christians. In neighbouring Near Eastern countries the official government was the Church-State authority of Byzantium. But Christians in Egypt, Syria and the borderlands of Arabia disagreed with the Byzantines, partly for reasons of local nationalism and also for theological reasons. Since the Great Councils of the Church, like that at Nicaea in 325 and that at Chalcedon in 451, the Eastern churches had been arguing about the doctrine of the Trinity.

One group, called Monophysites, was unable to accept that Jesus was fully man; another group, called Nestorians, was unable to accept that manhood and Godhead could be combined in Jesus. It was against the background of such arguments, and worse still against the background of Byzantine persecution of these sects, that the simple creed of Islam was preached. Muslims were taught to see Jesus as a human prophet and to regard the doctrine of the Trinity as a blasphemy against the One-ness of God. Even if early Muslims had been in closer contact with Christians they would have been unlikely to hear a calm and careful exploration of the mystery of the three-personal aspects of the One God; Christians were too interested in sectarian definitions, and did not take the Muslims' objections seriously.

Muslims' Faith in the One God

Although the *hanīfs*, the Jews and the Christians may have helped to raise questions in the minds of the idolatrous pagans of Arabia, they did not provide an appealing answer. Muslims look back to pre-Islamic Arabia and call it the 'Age of Ignorance' (*Jāhilīyah*). There were so many different cults, so many gods, goddesses, spirits and powers to appease, so many different places of worship, that men were confused and had no real sense of the overall power of God. Men could imagine that they were winning a short-term gift of divine favour by offering a sacrifice to the spirit of a cave, a tree, a well or a stone; they could go on a pilgrimage to one of the goddesses of Mecca; but before the great issues of life and death they felt helpless.

The Qur'ān describes this mentality in Sūrah 45, verse 23:

They say, 'There is nothing but our life in this world.
We live and we die, and it is only Time that destroys us'.

This sort of fatalism left no room for the idea of a life after death, and for God's reward for good and punishment for wrong. Instead, pre-Islamic society took judgement and justice into its own hands. If a murder took place, the victim's clan or tribe would set out on a bloodthirsty vendetta and take many lives in reprisal; and this would lead to reprisals from the other side. Female infants were sometimes buried alive, and women had very little protection. Against all this Muhammad protested, teaching that God is judge of all our actions and that we are answerable for what we do. Because God is just, man must be just. Because God is powerful and merciful, man can be guided and helped.

One part of the Muslim's faith in God is the way in which he affirms it in his confession of faith, 'There is no god but God'. Here he is saying 'Yes' to the way in which God has created the universe, is ruling it and will judge it. He is also saying 'Yes' to man's ability to recognize God's gifts and to accept man's dependence upon God as his servant. At the same time the Muslim is saying 'No' to the idea that there are any other gods or that there is any area of life or death where God is not Lord. The idols of Mecca were seen as of no value and were to be destroyed by the Muslims. But other false values were also being challenged by the summons to faith in One God. If men had made 'a god' out of their greed for wealth or out of their fanatical attachment to their tribe, they were now made to see that what was demanded of them was God's service and his alone.

The Nature of the One God

So far we have seen the way in which Muslims recognize God's unique power in creating, sustaining and judging the world. All this is implied when they say 'God is One', or 'There is no god but God'. Yet we have also seen that adjectives like 'merciful' and 'just' are used to describe God. These are among the 99 'most beautiful names' of God which help men to understand God's nature. Muslims regard the essence of God as essentially beyond man's knowledge, but they believe that God is one who communicates and demonstrates his nature to man. The words which are used to describe the various aspects or 'attributes' of God are words which are recognizable and understandable from a human point of view. Thus one can speak of Muslims worshipping a 'personal' God.

The names of God are not only used to describe him, but they are also used to address him. We shall see that the life of prayer is extremely important for the Muslim. This communication between man and God is possible because God reveals his nature to man and creates man with the ability to respond in service and worship. In the next chapter we shall see how Muslims perceive this channel of God's revelation of his nature and his will to man.

God's Claims on All Men

Islam is a faith for all men, of every race, language and background. It has spread from Arabia to every continent, especially Asia and Africa. Approximately one fifth of the world's population are Muslims, but Muslims believe that God is Lord of all, and they try to spread their preaching still wider. This preaching does not involve forcing men to believe, for the Qur'ān states in Sūrah 2, verse 257, that 'There is no compulsion in religion'. Nevertheless the Muslim is bound to defend his faith against any enemies.

God is seen as in control of all history. Men in every generation and in every place depend on him. The signs of the created world and the words of the many different prophets should remind man that he comes from God and that he will return to God for reward or punishment in accordance with how he has fulfilled his duty to God and his fellow men. Muslims believe that the clearest guidance to this human responsibility is to be found in the Qur'ān, the words which Muhammad experienced as coming to him from God.

2

THE HOLY QUR'ĀN

Muhammad's Experience

During the last twenty-two years of his life the Prophet Muhammad had successive vivid experiences in which he heard what he recognized as the words of God being spoken to him by the angel Gabriel. At first he distrusted these experiences, and was even tempted to commit suicide lest he be under some wicked delusion or, as an early biographer says, 'like a soothsayer or a man possessed — the two most hated categories of men to Muhammad'. He was encouraged to believe that he had had a genuine religious experience when his wife, Khadījah, and a Christian kinsman, Waraqah, insisted that God would not allow a good man to be misled and that Muhammad's experience was just like that of Moses when he had heard God's word addressed to him.

The words which Muhammad heard were memorized by him and were then dictated to a scribe or scribes. According to the early Muslim accounts, and also according to an allusion in the Qur'ān itself, the Prophet was unable to read or write himself. The words of the Qur'ān came to him at any time and in any place, and sometimes the scribe had nothing to write them on except a scrap of leather, palm-leaf or whitened bone of an animal. These fragments were all treasured and were regarded as quite distinct from any other of the Prophet's teachings.

The word Qur'ān means 'recitation' and it comes from the same root as the word *Iqra'*, 'Recite!', which most Muslims believe to have been the very first word which Muhammad heard as divine revelation. This word stands at the beginning of Sūrah 96, which goes on to speak in verse 4 of 'the Lord who taught with the pen'. This suggests the great Semitic notion of God's revealing scriptures to men, and we have just seen how Muhammad and those close to him compared his experience with that of Moses. It is very important to remember that Muslims do not believe that Muhammad wrote the Qur'ān, but that he found it 'written on his heart' by the angel Gabriel, to use a phrase from an early Muslim account.

The Text of the Qur'ān

We have established that Muslims do not speak of Muhammad's writing the Qur'ān, but of his receiving and reciting it. Just as Muhammad himself was conscious of the very special character of the Qur'ānic text, so those Muslims after him took pains to preserve with complete accuracy all the fragments of the Qur'ān. Only two years after Muhammad's death, with the further loss in battle of some of those who had already memorized the Qur'ān, the various fragments were collected. They were put together in what appears to many scholars to be a random order. Thus some of the latest to be revealed stand first, and some of the earliest stand towards the end. Some Muslims see a logical order in the apparently arbitrary arrangement; others regard the non-chronological order as a reminder to the reader that, although the Book was revealed within history and refers at points to events in Muhammad's lifetime, nevertheless the text is eternal. It is generally believed that the Prophet himself decreed into which chapter each verse should go.

A few years later, in the reign of Uthmān, the third caliph to rule the Muslims after Muhammad's death, a final check was made on the text of the Qur'ān. We can tell how careful and scrupulous the early Muslims were by the fact that even variations in pronunciation from one part of the Muslim world to another were disapproved of in the context of reciting the Qur'ān; and so the official text was established in accordance with the dialect of Mecca, and most other versions were destroyed by command of the caliph. Thus we can feel confident that the Qur'ān which we have today is as far as is humanly possible the text which was established within a few years of the Prophet's death.

Translations of the Qur'ān

The official Muslim position was for many centuries that the Qur'ān should not be translated. The Arabic meaning was explained, however, in the various languages used in the non-Arabic-speaking parts of the Islamic world. In modern times 'versions' or 'interpretations' have been authorized in European languages and in languages like Urdu or Swahili which many Muslims speak. These are regarded as giving only an approxi-

16

2. An illuminated copy of the Qur'ān

mate rendering of the original, and the Muslim worshipper must still use the Arabic text for devotional purposes.

Thus, in every part of the Muslim world, children are taught to memorize the Arabic words of the Qur'ān from an early age. They may not understand the Arabic language but they are taught the meaning of the words they learn. Some teenagers master the hundreds of pages of Arabic text and are then honoured with the title of *ḥāfiz* or 'memorizer'. Blind people are often trained to become *ḥāfiz*, and are thus equipped with a very useful profession in Islamic society.

One reason why translations have not taken the place of the original Arabic is that no translation can preserve the exact meaning of the original. Another reason is that much of the poetic beauty of the original must be lost in a translation. The Qur'ān makes its impact not only by the inspiring nature of its subject matter for Muslims, but also by its eloquence. In the Prophet Muhammad's own lifetime he was asked to produce a miracle which would prove to the disbelieving that he really was a prophet of God. Muhammad pointed to the Qur'ān as the miracle which proved the validity of his mission. Not only had its words been revealed to an 'illiterate' man, but the Arabic was so beautiful that he defied anyone to imitate it; when the odd enemies took up this challenge they failed miserably to match up to the beauty of the Qur'ān.

17

A Suggestion as to How to Read the Qur'ān in Translation

One must bear in mind the limitations of any translation of the Qur'ān, but for many people this will be their only chance to be exposed to the Qur'ān. It is important to start with a good translation, and in this connection the poetic qualities of A. J. Arberry's *The Koran Interpreted* are recommended; this is also a very scholarly and sensitive translation. Even when you have chosen your translation, there is the question as to where you should begin. Few students find it easy to start at the beginning and to move steadily to the end.

Despite what has already been said about the way in which this is an eternal text for the Muslim, it may help the newcomer to approach the text in a roughly chronological order. In this way the reader may try to respond to the impact of the *sūrahs* (chapters) and verses in the same sequence as it is probable that Muhammad himself received them. One might start with the beginning of Sūrah 96:

> Recite: In the Name of thy Lord who created,
> created man of a blood-clot.
> Recite: And thy Lord is the Most Generous,
> who taught by the Pen,
> taught Man that he knew not.
>
> No indeed; surely Man waxes insolent,
> for he thinks himself self-sufficient.
> Surely unto thy Lord is the Returning.

Another passage considered among the very first to be received is the beginning of Sūrah 74; God is addressing Muhammad again:

> O thou shrouded in thy mantle,
> arise and warn!
> Thy Lord magnify
> thy robes purify
> and defilement flee!
> Give not, thinking to gain greater
> and be patient unto thy Lord.
>
> For when the Trump is sounded
> that day will be a harsh day,
> for the unbelievers not easy.

Having read these and others of the brief *sūrahs* at the end of the Qur'ān, such as 82, 84, 93, 101 and 112, you may proceed to some of the great narrative passages. The story of the birth of Jesus is given in Sūrah 19, verses 16–34; there is the long story of Joseph in Sūrah 12. The way in which these stories are told is full of pointers to God's mercy to men and to God's claims upon men. The legal implications of this are worked out in some of the longest *sūrahs* like Sūrah 4, 'The Women', which includes much family legislation, as does Sūrah 2.

One of the best ways to sample these later and longer *sūrahs* is to use the index at the end of a translation and to look up subjects of interest to yourself, for example: Abraham; Arabic; the Book; Creation; Divorce; Food laws; Hypocrites; Jesus; Jews; Marriage; Muhammad; Orphans; Paradise; Parents; Prayer; Resurrection; Satan; (Holy) War. If you follow up some of these theological or sociological issues or subjects you will begin to feel the impact of the Qur'ān upon the whole of Islamic history.

Man's Duty to God in the Qur'ān

Muslims often sum up their main duties towards God under the heading of 'The Five Pillars of the Faith'. The Qur'ān itself does not use this exact phrase, but it does refer to all the five pillars. Of these the first, confessing that God is One and that Muhammad is his Prophet, has already been mentioned; it is the basic step whereby one becomes a Muslim. If this first pillar seems a relatively easy duty, remember that it is not just the saying of a formula but the deliberate meaning of the confession of faith that is important. There is an interesting passage in Sūrah 49 verses 14–15 where desert Arabs claim to have faith but are told 'Faith has not yet entered your hearts', and they are reminded that the test of faith is in actions.

The most important ritual action for the Muslim is the duty to pray to God five times each day. The Qur'ān uses the word *ṣalāt* for this five-times daily formal prayer, and the word *du'ā'* or 'supplication' is used for additional prayers. The precise regulations about the ritual prayer are not given in the Qur'ān, but Muhammad built on the basic Qur'ānic principles. The times for prayer are between dawn and sunrise, after midday, before sunset, between sunset and the fading of red from the sky, and at night. Sūrah 30, verses 17–18 gives general guidance on this. Before prayer the Muslim must wash his face, hands and arms, and feet. As he offers his prayer he uses not only his tongue but the whole of his body, facing towards Mecca (the *qiblah* or direction), bending, bowing and finally fully prostrating himself. The requirement to pray is lifted only in the context of children or the mentally deficient. One catechism says that children should be taught to pray from the age of seven and are required to pray

3. Muslims in the Nusret Djahan Mosque in Denmark face towards Mecca

regularly from the age of ten. *Salāt* may be offered in the mosque or anywhere else. For men it is preferable to pray in a mosque (if available) while it is preferable for women to pray at home (though permissible in the mosque). On a Friday at midday, prayer should be in the mosque and a sermon should be preached to the congregation.

The Qur'ān frequently couples with the requirement of *ṣalāt* the requirement of *zakāt*, ritual almsgiving. This coupling of a spiritual and a social duty is like the combination of faith and good works of which the Qur'ān also frequently speaks. In Sūrah 2, verses 171–3, one reads that it is not 'true piety' simply to turn one's face in a particular direction in prayer:

> True piety is this:
> to believe in God, and the Last Day,
> the angels, the Book, and the Prophets,
> to give of one's substance, however cherished,,
>   to kinsmen, and orphans,
> the needy, the traveller, beggars,
>   and to ransom the slave,
> to perform the prayer (*ṣalāt*), to pay the alms (*zakāt*).

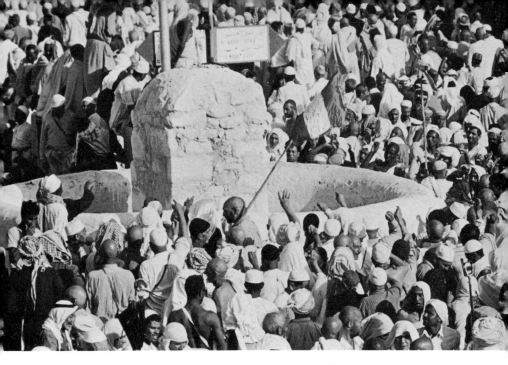

4. Pilgrims throw stones at one of the three huge pillars at Mina

The categories of those in need as mentioned in this passage are the basic beneficiaries for the alms tax (which amounts to one fortieth of one's moveable surplus income or savings). There is also the Qur'ānic summons to give additional free-will offerings known as *ṣadaqāt*.

The fourth pillar is that of fasting, prescribed in Sūrah 2, verses 179–183. The healthy adult Muslim is called upon to fast from dawn to sunset for every day of the month of Ramaḍān. Since this is a lunar month it falls back each annual season and may fall in the hottest or the coldest time of the year, when the days are at their longest or at their shortest. Special arrangements are made in extreme latitudes. It is a tough discipline to abstain from all food and drink, but devout Muslims find great spiritual enrichment from this observance.

Finally the Qur'ān bids all Muslims who can afford it and who are in good health to go on pilgrimage to Mecca once in their lifetime. Mecca is not only the focal point in Islamic history, but is regarded by Muslims as associated also with Adam who built there a shrine, the Ka'bah, which was rebuilt after the Flood by Abraham and Ishmael, to whom the angel Gabriel gave the Black Stone (a meteorite) to include in the shrine. Muslims on pilgrimage walk round the Ka'bah and kiss the Black Stone,

5. The pilgrims of all nations near the Mount of Arafat in the background — during the pilgrimage

as well as carrying out many other ceremonies (most of them commemorative of Abraham, Hagar & Ishmael) as demonstrated by the Prophet Muhammad. In the modern days with chartered planes and ships, hundreds of thousands of Muslims gather at the annual pilgrimage time and present a stirring picture of the international nature of Islam. Non-Muslims are not allowed in the cities of Mecca and Medina.

Man's Duty to Man in the Qur'ān

Among the five pillars of the faith we have already seen, notably with zakāt, that a man's duty to God gives him responsibilities towards his fellow men. The Qur'ān contains a considerable amount of social legislation, or, more accurately, the basic principles upon which Muslims could work out a fuller system of legislation. Muslims are to approach God by the path (sharī'ah) of the law. This sharī'ah does not only cover public and private law, but it covers the ritual requirements which have been discussed above, and it extends to cover all ethical and personal decisions and actions ranging from one's kindness to those in trouble to how one should clean one's teeth.

In the area of public law the Qur'ān lays down severe punishments for theft; Sūrah 5, verse 42, says that a deliberate and malicious thief should have a hand cut off. Adultery is to be punished by a virtually fatal flogging (see Sūrah 24, verse 2) for both the offending man and the offending woman, provided that there is voluntary confession or four reliable eye-witnesses to confirm the crime. Retaliation for murder or injury must be on a strictly equitable basis (see Sūrah 2, verse 273). Commercial law is given a new dignity with the requirement to be lenient in recovering debts, and in the requirement for contracts to be written in order to avoid disputes (see Sūrah 2, verses 282–284). The Qur'ān, Sūrah 2, verse 276, also prohibits usury, and this has often prevented the exploitation of poor by rich; as in any culture, however, a law may sometimes be broken more often than it is observed.

In the area of private law the Qur'ān makes fairly detailed rulings about marriage and divorce. One of the most famous verses is Sūrah 4, verse 3, which allows more than one wife in certain circumstances, notably complete equality between the wives, a concern for widows and orphans, and a limit of four wives:

> If you fear that you will not act justly
> towards the orphans, marry such women
> as seem good to you, two, three, four;
> but if you fear you will not be equitable
> then only one . . . .

In modern practice most Muslims outside Africa take only one wife. Divorce legislation in the Qur'ān includes the provision of a four-month waiting period before a divorce can be accepted; compensation for the wife is also mentioned, particularly in terms of her keeping the marriage dowry, which in Islamic custom is paid by the man to the woman. Women are also provided for in the inheritance laws, whereas only males had benefitted in pre-Islamic society. Other Qur'ānic passages such as Sūrah 2, verse 235, and Sūrah 29, verse 7, lay down the care which parents must take of their children, and the care and obedience which children must show to their parents.

The Qur'ān also includes various other laws, such as the prohibition of pork, wine and gambling.

6. General view showing the pilgrimage on arrival at Mecca — turning around the Ka'bah

3

THE PROPHET MUHAMMAD

The Role of the Prophet

The religious tradition of Islam was until recently often called Muhammadanism in English-speaking countries. This was a bad title because it suggested that Muslims worshipped Muhammad. They revere him deeply and they regard his life as a model life; but they do not worship him. This book started with chapters about Muslims' faith in God and about the Holy Qur'ān because Muslims take their basic point of departure from the conviction that God communicates with mankind through revealed scriptures. The function of the prophet is to relay these scriptures to man.

Christians and Muslims both talk of God's attribute of speech and communication as 'The Word of God' (*kalām Allāh*). Christians believe that this communicative faculty of God was expressed in the man Jesus, in his words, his actions, his life, death and resurrection; Christians speak therefore of 'The Word made Flesh'. Muslims feel that this doctrine is a heresy against the concept of the One-ness of God and they believe that the eternal Truth of God breaks into history not in the form of a man's life but in the form of revealed scripture; this is close to a doctrine of 'The Word made Book'.

As we approach the life of Muhammad we should remember that he was, both in his self-understanding and in Muslims' doctrines, an ordinary man in terms of his birth and daily life and death. But he was not an ordinary man in the way in which he experienced God's revealing to him of the Qur'ān and God's guiding him in all his actions and teachings. We shall see that it was only in the later years of his life that he came to realize this mission as a prophet of God, and that slowly but surely his fellow

7. General view of the Holy City of Mecca with the Ka'bah, around which the pilgrims walk seven times before they start saying their prayers or request favours from God

countrymen recognized his mission. But Muslims believe that his whole life was divinely guided and sinless just as they believe this to be the case with all the other prophets, like Moses and Jesus, who preceded him; in the case of Jesus Muslims also believe that he was born of a virgin, that he performed miracles, that God spared him from dying on the cross, and (in orthodox exegesis) that he ascended to heaven and will come again to earth before the Last Judgement. The great miracle of Muhammad's life remains the fact that he received the Qur'ān, and that thereby, possessing what Muslims regard as the full and complete scriptures, he is the last prophet for mankind.

Muhammad's Early Life

Muhammad was born in 570 A.D., just after the death of his father, and when his mother died six years later he was left an orphan. He was brought up by his grandfather and then by his uncle, Abū Ṭālib. His family was not wealthy, nor was it depressed. He was involved in work with the trading caravans that plied to and from his native city of Mecca. On one trip to Syria, when he was about twelve years old, he was singled out from the other men in the caravan and recognized by a hermit monk, Baḥīrā, as bearing 'the seal of prophecy'. This story reminds one of the way in which the young David was recognized and anointed by Samuel.

Other indications of Muhammad's impressive piety as a young man include the fact that he was chosen to be the husband of a wealthy widow, Khadījah, with whom he lived happily from his twenty-fifth year; four daughters survived. In his thirty-fifth year we hear of Muhammad's being chosen to resolve a dispute between the clans of the tribe of Quraysh as to which clan should have the honour to replace the Black Stone during the restoration of the Ka'bah. He appointed each clan's chief to hold a corner of a cloak while he lifted the stone on to the cloak. But neither he nor others recognized any special religious or social authority in him until he was forty years old.

Muhammad's Call to Prophethood

It was Muhammad's practice to leave the city of Mecca, with its busy commercial life and its pilgrimage and caravan traffic, and to go out into the surrounding hills to meditate. In the year 610 A.D. he had gone to a cave on Mount Ḥirā and, while asleep, he experienced the sensation of being pressed hard by the angel Gabriel and being summoned to 'Recite!'. He resisted the summons at first, and in desperation to escape, he wanted to hurl himself down the mountain. The angel reassured him, and so did his family when he told them of what had happened.

The same sort of experience was repeated in different situations and Muhammad came to accept it and to believe that he was being called by God to be a prophet, to warn men of the way that God would judge their lives and would reward or punish them according to their deeds. At this stage Muhammad shared this message only with close friends and associates, and gathered a band of followers who were later called the early 'Companions of the Prophet'.

It was not until 613 A.D. that Muhammad undertook his first public preaching, and very quickly he fell foul of the Meccans who regarded the preaching of a life after death as folly, and who feared that the preaching of the One God would undercut their profitable pilgrimage traffic to the shrines of the Meccan goddesses, Manāt, Allāt and al-'Uzzā.

Opposition to the Early Muslims

The Prophet himself had to face mockery and interruptions to his preaching, but he was not ill-treated physically except once or twice. This was largely because his uncle Abū Ṭālib and his clan the Banū Hāshim protected him. There were less fortunate Muslims like the negro slave

Bilāl (an example of the inter-racial nature of Islam from its early days). Bilāl was taken by his Meccan master and beaten, imprisoned and then weighed down with a great stone on his chest and exposed to the heat of the desert sun. Yet through all his sufferings he would not give up his faith in God, and lay there groaning 'One! One!'.

In 615 A.D. some of the new Muslims decided that the Christian kingdom of Abyssinia across the Red Sea would be more hospitable to the young faith of Islam. But Muhammad and his closest 'Companions' remained in Mecca. From 616 A.D. they had to face a boycott of the clan of the Banū Hāshim to which Muhammad belonged; this meant that trade and marriage with other clans were forbidden. Muhammad became even more threatened and unprotected when his uncle Abū Ṭalib and his wife Khadījah both died in the year 619 A.D.

The Emigration to Medina

While Muhammad's fortunes seemed to be at a very low ebb he was encouraged by certain spiritual experiences. He felt that he was carried miraculously from Mecca to Jerusalem by night, and that while there he was taken up to heaven and greeted by the other prophets of history before being conducted before the Throne of God and instructed in the ritual of prayer. We have a less dramatic, but none the less moving, account of the Prophet's spiritual determination at this stage of Meccan opposition. His biographer, Ibn Isḥāq, records the following prayer of Muhammad:

O God, to Thee I complain of my weakness . . .
Thou art the Lord of the weak, and Thou art
my Lord . . . If Thou art not angry with me,
I care not . . . There is no power and no might
save in Thee.

Muhammad had no immediate prospects of winning wider support at Mecca, and so it was a great new opportunity when Muhammad was invited to leave Mecca and to go north some 300 miles to the city of Yathrib (shortly to be renamed Madīnat al-nabī, the 'City of the Prophet'; in English this is written as Medina). As early as 620 A.D. there had been six converts to Islam from among the inhabitants of Yathrib who had come on pilgrimage to Mecca; twelve more converts professed Islam the following year, and in 622 A.D. there were as many as seventy-five of these converts (now called 'Helpers') who urged Muhammad and his 'Companions' to emigrate to Yathrib. This emigration was called the *Hijrah* (sometimes written in English as 'hegira') and it provides the starting year for the Muslim calendar, so that Muslim dates are expressed, in lunar years, with 1 A.H. (*anno hegirae*) equivalent to 622 A.D. (*anno domini*).

The Community at Medina

One reason why the 'Helpers' had urged Muhammad to emigrate was that their city had been going through a very troubled time with fierce tensions and even open warfare between the local clans and tribes. In these circumstances Muhammad was welcomed as a judge or arbitrator. He succeeded in uniting the various Arab clans and the local Jewish settlers into one community or 'federation' (*ummah* in Arabic). Instead of disputes being referred to the violent vendettas of tribal ethics, they were now to be referred to the Prophet and to God. Religious authority had overtaken tribal authority. It is important to notice that this religious authority was established at Medina without any appeal to military strength, for it depended rather on the magnetic appeal of Muhammad himself and on his preaching of men's duty to God and to each other.

If the formative ideas of the community at Medina were the authority of God and his Prophet and the ideal of a united local community, the Muslims were soon bound to look further afield. Medina, like Mecca, depended for her prosperity on the passing caravan trade, from which taxes were exacted. Meccans were now plotting against Muhammad and therefore the Meccan caravans were regarded as fair game for raiding and reconnaissance expeditions from Medina. When the Meccans retaliated in 624 A.D., their 950 men faced the small Muslim army of 238 'Helpers' and 86 'Immigrants' (as the Meccan 'Companions' were now known). Muslims regard the eventual victory of Muhammad at the Battle of Badr as a miraculous mark of God's favour, and as a turning point in Islamic history.

The fighting with Meccan expeditions was to continue over succeeding years. It is interesting to measure the increasing success of the Muslims by the way in which Muhammad can send increasingly large armies against the Meccans. These expeditions also illustrate the way in which much of this support was coming from tribes outside Medina. The allegiance of some of these tribes was strengthened by Muhammad's taking wives for himself from them. These marriages, as well as other marriages to widows of men who had died fighting for Islam, helped the Prophet's prestige; he was granted a special dispensation to take these additional wives, of whom there were ten after Khadījah.

One of Muhammad's chief difficulties at Medina was the way in which some of the Jewish tribes who had originally joined the *ummah* came to be suspected of treachery. Although the Qur'ān speaks with high regard of Jews and Christians, especially Christians, there were clashes with various Jewish tribes. In 624 A.D., the Banū Qaynuqā' were expelled from their lands after persistent trouble-making and eventually insulting a Muslim woman; the following year the Banū Naḍīr were expelled on the charge of a plot; in 627 A.D. the Banū Qurayẓah were punished according to tribal and Jewish law for their treachery — the men were executed and the women enslaved. It is noticeable that this hard sentence was not passed by Muhammad but the Arab chief whose clan loyalty they had offended.

The Fall of Mecca

For several years Muhammad seems to have had much more to engage his attention in Medina, but it is clear that he had not forgotten Mecca. In 628 A.D. he agreed to a treaty with the Meccans, the treaty of al-Huday-bīyah, which enabled him and the Muslims to go on pilgrimage to Mecca in the following year. The Meccans evacuated their city for this 'Lesser Pilgrimage' (so called to distinguish it from the greater pilgrimage or *hajj*). Several important citizens of Mecca became Muslim at this time, and this may have paved the way for the events of the following year.

On 11th January 630 A.D., the Prophet Muhammad returned to Mecca with 10,000 men. The city submitted to him without any bloodshed and there was a general amnesty declared. The Prophet formally ordered that the idols in the city should be destroyed, and it was on this occasion that Sūrah 17, verse 82, was revealed:

The truth has come, and falsehood has vanished away;
　　surely falsehood
is ever certain to vanish.

Some of the surrounding tribes appear to have interpreted the bloodless capitulation of Mecca as a sign of weakness, and as many as 20,000 of the tribes of Thaqīf and Hawāzin were hovering, vulture-like, outside Mecca. Muhammad turned on them and defeated them at the Battle of Hunayn. This victory and the generous terms granted were noticed by other tribes and there was now a great addition of tribal support to Muhammad. In October 630 A.D. we hear of the Muslims having 30,000 men and 10,000 horses to face a skirmish at Tābūk with the army of the Byzantine Emperor, who, in common with other world rulers, had received an invitation to become Muslim — invitations which were at that stage declined.

Muhammad as a Ruler

We have seen evidence for the growing military and political authority of Muhammad, culminating in his being ready to confront the great empires of his day. But this should not obscure his essentially religious role and motivation. We have seen too how he himself rejected the tribal ethic of revenge and reprisal in many instances and how this led to a great mass movement of Arabs into the 'household of faith'.

This religious role of Muhammad is illustrated by a story which his biographer Ibn Ishāq tells. Just before the Prophet's last and fatal illness (aggravated by poison from an aggrieved Jewess), he was walking with a friend in the cemetery, and he prayed and spoke as follows:

> Peace be upon you, people of the graves. Happy are
> you . . . (He then told his friend) I have been given
> the choice between the keys of the treasuries of
> this world and long life here followed by paradise,
> or meeting my Lord and paradise (at once).

When the friend urged Muhammad to choose to stay alive and preside over the further expansion of Islam (which the next chapter will describe), he declined, and said that he preferred to die, to return as soon as possible to his Lord.

The sincerity and humility which had been with Muhammad at the outset of his mission are seen as remaining to the end of his life in 632 A.D. It was a life which subsequent Muslims were to record and to strive to imitate in every detail.

4

THE COMMUNITY OF MUSLIMS

The Spread of Islam

We have just seen that one of the great achievements of Muhammad was to bring men and women together into a community. He did this first on a small scale in face of opposition and persecution in Mecca; then he brought reconciliation between the warring factions of Medina; finally he won over the Meccans and the tribes of Arabia. As soon as he died some of these tribes tried to break away in a rebellion known as the *Riddah*; in particular they refused to pay the alms tax (*zakāt*), which was one of the 'pillars' of Islamic faith. These tribes thought that Muhammad's death would mean the end of the community, but they were quickly shown that their loyalty had not been to Muhammad just as if he were another tribal chief; their loyalty should be to God.

Some of Muhammad's closest followers could not believe that he was dead and it was Abū Bakr, the first 'caliph' (deputy or successor), who reminded them as follows:

> Let whoever worships Muhammad know that Muhammad
> is dead; but let whoever worships God know that
> the Lord lives and does not die.

The Muslims of Medina and Mecca accepted that their loyalty to God and to the memory of the Prophet meant that they should obey the new caliph, and that under him the Islamic community could continue to thrive and spread. The rebellious tribes returned to their obedience as Muslims. Abū Bakr's swift and successful checking of any breakaway tendencies enabled immediate expansion beyond Arabia. We shall see that it was an expansion which was made *initially* possible by the military brilliance of the Arab generals. But it was an expansion which led to an *eventually* permanent empire and religion only by a long and patient process of developing the community.

The Military Achievement

There was a time when a chapter like this would have been summed up with the phrase 'Islam was spread by the sword'. This is a dangerous over-simplification. We have noted already the Qur'ānic verse which forbids 'compulsion' in religion. When Islam spread rapidly over much of the civilized world it spread first as a military and political success story; yet it was sometimes centuries before the inhabitants of the conquered lands voluntarily became Muslims. On the other hand the motive in the minds of the caliphs behind the military and political expansion was that ultimately there should be these conversions to Islam; in the minds of the soldiers, as in every other generation, there was the desire for the spoils of war, but the Muslim conquests were remarkable for their discipline and lack of wanton destruction.

Already under Abū Bakr the Muslim armies were sent out to defeat the Byzantine army in Syria. One Muslim army had to carry out a five-day forced march across a waterless desert, killing their camels on the way to drink their bodies' reserves of water. When Abū Bakr died in the same year as this victory, 634 A.D., he was succeeded by 'Umar, who, during the next ten years presided over the defeat of Syria, Egypt and Persia in rapid succession. At the decisive battle over the Byzantines in Syria in 636 A.D., the Muslims were urged into battle by the river Yarmuk with the summons:

Paradise is before you; the devil and hell fire are behind you!

After the collapse and departure of the Byzantine army it is interesting to note the reaction of the native Christian population of a Syrian town like Homs:

We like your rule and justice much better than the condition of oppression and tyranny under which we have been living.

In 637 A.D., another of 'Umar's generals won a great victory over the emperor of Sasanid Persia; the Muslims took a great treasure but permitted the emperor to escape; once again the local Christians welcomed their new over-lords in place of the persecutions of the Zoroastrian court of Persia. Within four years the whole of Mesopotamia was under Muslim control, and within another ten years vast areas of Persia too. The fact that it was a Persian slave who murdered 'Umar in 644 A.D. should be seen as a personal grudge, although it is also a pointer to the way in which Persia was only slowly Islamized and the way in which it was always tending to political independence from the Arab centre.

In Egypt the indigenous Christian population, with their Monophysite leanings, were glad to shake off the Byzantine authority and to replace the puppet Patriarch with their own exiled Patriarch. After the Muslims' first successes in driving out the Byzantines by 641 A.D., the Byzantines returned in 645 A.D., the second year of the caliphate of 'Uthmān. The Egyptian Christian Copts helped the Muslims to repulse the Byzantines then and on several occasions in the next ten years, notably in final naval victories over the Byzantines. It is remarkable how versatile were these early Muslim generals in their ability to exchange the camel, the 'ship of the desert', for the naval galleys of the Mediterranean. From civilized Egypt the Muslims spread rapidly into nomadic (and residually Christian) North Africa, and thence into Spain and, temporarily, even France. On the Eastern front Muslim armies soon entered India and all this within 100 years from the death of Muhammad.

The Organization of the Community

It was not only military brilliance which led to the expansion of Islam. The problem with a world empire is how to administer it, and in this the Muslims were remarkably efficient, largely because they were prepared to take over and to preserve good features from previous administrations of Byzantines and Sasanids while at the same time they introduced new integrating focal points of their own. There were the new camp cities which they built to house their armies, thus keeping them away from damaging civilians' property. There was a basically fair taxation system whereby, eventually, everyone paid tax on their land (this tax was called *kharāj*). Christians and Jews paid in addition a poll-tax (*jizyah*) but did not have to do military service or pay the Muslims' alms-tax.

The chief focal point for the new community was, however, their allegiance to Islam, whether they were Arabs or newly converted non-Arabs. And yet there was no centralized religious hierarchy separate from the political administration. Islam has not had a priesthood in the sense of there being certain men with special spiritual authority; the caliph at the head of the community, and the judges and governors under him, have combined political and spiritual authority over Muslims. We saw at the outset of this book that Muslims do not recognize any ultimate distinction between the sacred and the secular, and so ideally the government of

Muslim countries should be worked out in relation to religious teachings.

It was the religious lawyers who interpreted the teachings of the Qur'ān and the Prophet in such a way that they could be applied to every-day life. It has been said:

No law is created, but no jurisprudence is uncreated.

A Muslim would probably believe this in the sense that the *Sharī*'ah, the Law of God, is regarded as being given by God to man and therefore is not subject to any alteration or innovation (*bid'ah*). On the other hand the application of this Law is by human obedience, interpretation and organization, and this is called jurisprudence. The lawyers or jurists of Islam are human; they are not infallible; but they do have great authority provided that they fulfil their responsibilities to God and to the community in accordance with various strict regulations.

The Schools of Law

Over the first two centuries of Islamic history men were appointed as caliphs, governors and judges, and they found that they were often faced with new situations in public law and in private law such as had not been apparent in the simple societies of Medina and Mecca in the lifetime of the Prophet. Sometimes they followed the practice or custom which existed in a particular part of the Muslim world; sometimes they used their own initiative and invented a new jurisprudential ruling. This led to an element of variety and inconsistency between different parts of the empire and even between different judges in the same place. Four basic rules were therefore agreed upon in order to prevent this confusion.

In the first place the authority of the Qur'ān was regarded as supreme, and where the Qur'ān gave a clear ruling on a question of public or private law that ruling could not be reversed. In many instances the Qur'ān is general rather than specific in its guidance, and so the jurist must then turn to the second basic principle, the teaching of the Prophet. Here the jurists were at first in greater difficulty than in the case of the Qur'ān; they had a standard text of the Qur'ān, but the teachings of the Prophet and the historical descriptions of his actions were not yet compiled in any recognized collection. The records of the Prophet's practice (*sunnah*) were until the third century of Islam in scattered and fragmentary written collections, and, supremely, in carefully preserved memories (oral tradition is very important in a pre-literate society, and it can be remarkably accurate). The jurists created the need for systematic and critical editions of the *sunnah* of the Prophet and the early 'Companions' and these collections are known as the 'Traditions' or *Hadīth* collections.

There are two other fundamental rules for Islamic jurisprudence (known as the *Usūl al-Fiqh*). One is 'consensus' of the community, whereby Muslims believe that 'the community will not agree in an error'; the other is 'analogy', whereby one must take decisions on a new issue, not in accordance with one's own fancies, but by strict reference to any previous comparable issue, notably in the Prophet's life. Together with the authority of the Qur'ān and *sunnah* these principles make for a common pattern of Islamic law all over the Muslim world. There are minor regional variations according to four major schools of law; the Hanafī school is strong in Turkey and North India and Pakistan; the Shāfi'ī school is strong in Lower Egypt, Syria, South India and South East Asia; the Mālikī school is found in North Africa and West Africa; the conservative Hanbalī school is found in Arabia. The schools take their names from famous early jurists who laid differing emphasis on various of the fundamental principles. But their followers agree to differ, and this provides a good basis for diversity in unity, for orthodoxy without compulsion.

Orthodox Theology as a Cement

In many ways the jurisprudence (*fiqh*), which has just been described, has played a more central part than theology (*kalām*) in holding together the Muslim world. The theologians of Islam have been more theoretical and philosophical, and less practical. And yet the next chapter will illustrate how some of the gravest threats to the unity and stability of the Muslim world came as religious threats from sects or heretics. And so it was important to establish a commonly agreed basis for belief which might hold together the whole wide community.

The caliph was the figurehead not only for the political unity of Islam, however difficult it might be to achieve such unity. He was, first and foremost, the figurehead for the way in which Islam held the Muslims together as one community under God. Even when independent dynasties began to break away from the political control of the central government, they went on swearing allegiance to the caliph; they went on sending rich gifts to the court of the caliph; they went on dreaming that the caliph might be strong enough to re-unite the provinces of the Islamic empire, provinces that had begun to break away from the second and third centuries of Islam onwards.

If the orthodox theologians desired a caliph to act as figurehead for the spiritual and political empire, they also desired that theology itself could act as a cement for the loyalty of the empire. We have seen that one ingredient in this cement was the 'agreement to differ' among the jurists; this allowed regional variations, but over-all unity. Another basic ingredient was the office of the caliph. Thirdly there was developed a sense of religious orthodoxy which cut through the various differences of interpretation that had arisen and that had caused divisions between sects.

The Orthodox Position

This sense of being orthodox or Sunnī was not maintained by reaching very precise definitions and answers to questions about God's relationship to man, and man's relationship to his fellow man. The Lordship of God and the obedient duty and servanthood of man were accepted as basic convictions or hypotheses 'without asking how'. This formula was particularly important for the most influential school of theologians, founded by al-Ash'arī, who died in 935 A.D. This school held that God had existed from eternity, and that while one must not take literally the idea of God's seeing, hearing, etc., one must not see these 'attributes' as simply metaphors, but as realities which are part of his 'essence'; one creed used by the Sunnīs speaks of the relationship of God's 'attributes' to his 'essence' in the following deliberate paradox: 'They are not He, nor are they other than He'. The orthodox position also accepted without question the belief that the Qur'ān is the Word of God, thereby rejecting the rationalist position, shortly to be described, which insisted that the Qur'ān was created in time. A third fundamental tenet of Ash'arite theology was that all men's acts are by God's 'decree', but that man has the responsibility for 'acquiring' what God has created for him. This doctrine of 'acquisition' was aimed at softening the harsh predestinarian doctrine that some sects had introduced. Fatalism remains very strong at a popular level in the Muslim world, but it is important to note that the Qur'ān with its preaching of God's justice rejects the idea of a capricious fate, and that orthodox theology also defends the idea of human responsibility.

5

THE CONTRIBUTION OF INDIVIDUALS
AND MINORITY GROUPS

The Role of the Individual in Sunnī Islam

We have just seen that it was the idea of the community which lay at the heart of the success of Islam and which was also formally safeguarded by the jurists' doctrine of 'consensus' and by the aspiration for universal 'orthodoxy'. The responsibility of the individual was thus seen as his support for the agreement already reached and accepted by the community. The individual, or group of individuals, was not to separate into a sectarian position; one must accept that 'the community does not agree in an error'. It was sometimes held that one must accept the official position 'without asking how'.

And yet there were many brilliant individuals in the Sunnī community who made their own particular contribution to the whole. We have already noted the way in which early caliphs gave fine leadership; in this connection one thinks especially of 'The Four Rightly Guided Caliphs', Abū Bakr (died 634 A.D.), 'Umar (died 644 A.D.), 'Uthmān (died 655 A.D.) and 'Alī (died 661 A.D.). Among the Umayyad caliphs who ruled from Damascus for the next ninety years, 'Umar ibn 'Abd al-'Azīz (died 720 A.D.) was especially admired by the orthodox. In the ensuing 'Abbasid caliphate (750–1258 A.D.) there were far fewer caliphs with a combination of spiritual and political authority, but there were many other individuals who made great personal contributions.

The Golden Age of Islam

We have noted the influence exerted by the founders of the four law schools: Abū Ḥanīfah (died 767 A.D.), Mālik ibn Anas (died 795 A.D.), al-Shāfi'ī (died 819 A.D.) and Aḥmad ibn Ḥanbal (died 855 A.D.). Then there were the authors of the great collections of Traditions: most famous among these were al-Bukhārī (died 870 A.D.) and Muslim (died 875 A.D.). The first century of the 'Abbāsid caliphate is sometimes known as the Golden Age of Islam partly because it saw the activity of these leaders often entitled Imām, e.g., *Imām* Mālik (although the word *imām* is also used for any religious leader, such as the *imām* of the local mosque). A further reason for the distinction of this period was that the political and economic stability and prosperity gave hospitable conditions for a considerable intellectual awakening in philosophy, science and theology. The caliphs became patrons of the arts and sciences; great libraries and academic institutions were built up; translations of Greek, Syriac and Sanskrit were commissioned.

It was the Muslims who encouraged this great influx of Greek, Christian, Hindu and Buddhist learning into centres like Baghdad. The 'Philosopher of the Arabs', al-Kindī (died 870 A.D.), accepted Aristotle's idea about the eternity of the universe, and he questioned the Muslim belief in the resurrection of the body; yet he held to belief in God, and still regarded the teaching of the Qur'ān as inspired by God. A group of rationalist philosophers of this period, known as the Mu'tazilites, also tried to use Greek concepts to explain Islamic theology. But they so insisted on the rational unity of God that they denied that God's 'attributes' were eternal, and tried to force people by a sort of 'inquisition' (*miḥnah*) to confess that the Qur'ān must be created, because only the 'essence' of God was uncreated. They were also unpopular because, like another group in early Islam (the Khārijites — who survive today in parts of Algeria, Tunisia, Muscat and Zanzibar) they said that God's justice demanded that all sinners should go to hell for all eternity; the orthodox held out hopes of divine reward as well as punishment for the repentant Muslim.

This had been a period of intellectual activity and sincerity, despite the abuses of 'inquisition' and orthodox 'counter-inquisition'. Yet the dangers of sectarianism led to many attempts to reconcile reason and revelation.

The Philosophers

After the early period of the translators (many of whom were Christians working for Muslim patrons), al-Kindī and the Mu'tazilites, we come to a series of great men who influenced not only the history of Islamic thinking but who are world figures. Al-Rāzī (died about 925 A.D.) won international fame as a medical scientist, with many editions of his work translated in the West; it was he who made decisive discoveries in the diagnosis and treatment of smallpox and measles; his portrait is in the medical faculty of the university of the Sorbonne in Paris. As a thinker he was regarded by some as irreligious by his suggesting the superiority of reason to revelation. Al-Fārābī (died 950 A.D.) tried to explain revelation in rational terms; the prophet was a sort of Platonic 'philosopher king' who, by great intellectual effort, philosophical distinction and spiritual imagination, could bridge the gulf between the limited human intellect and the infinite Truth of Divine intellect; he regarded God as 'necessarily existent' in order to be the 'First Cause' from which all creation was to issue or 'emanate'.

One of the most famous philosophers was Ibn Sīnā (died 1037 A.D. and known in Europe as Avicenna). He was a master of the following subjects by the age of seventeen: the Qur'ān, jurisprudence, Aristotelian logic, science, medicine, philosophy! He read Aristotle's *Metaphysica* forty times and was still troubled by it, until he found the Islamic answer in al-Fārābī! For Ibn Sīnā, the issue was not so much to reconcile reason with revelation as to see that revelation must be added to reason if the whole truth were to be explored. Beyond the 'reasonable religion' of the theologians and philosophers lay the symbolism and metaphor of 'light and darkness', 'Stranger and Guide', 'angels' etc. He accepted reason, but saw its limitations and the consequent need for myth, poetic language and symbol. The Christian West made use of his rationalistic proofs for the necessarily existent God; the East valued in particular his more gnostic approach to the idea of Truth as an inexplicable but nevertheless explorable mystery.

The Mystics

In reaction against the legalism of some of the jurists, and against the arrogant rationalism of some of the philosophers, a very important movement developed in early Islamic society. Muslims remembered the simplicity of the life of Muhammad and the absence of dogmatic argumentation from his preaching. Individuals and groups who were called ṣūfīs began to opt out of the legal and theological wrangles of the second and third century of Islam, and withdrew into the simple life of ascetics and into the devotional practices of mystics.

The word ṣūfī may refer to the ṣūf or scratchy wool which some of these men and women wore next to the skin to remind them that spiritual concerns are more important than physical pleasures; or the word may refer to a similar Arabic word meaning 'purity'. Famous early ṣūfīs included the woman Rābi'ah (died 801 A.D.); one day, when asked why she was running with fire in one hand and a bucket of water in the other, she exclaimed:

I am going to light a fire in Heaven and pour water on Hell, so that both obstacles may disappear.

She insisted that God should be worshipped for his own sake, and not for hope of reward or for fear of punishment.

Some ṣūfīs developed the idea of the *unity* of God into the idea of the possibility of man's achieving *union* with God. Sometimes this was expressed in careful and acceptable terms, such as those used by al-Junayd (died 908 A.D.) who spoke of the believer as 'sunk in the flooding seas of God's unity'. Sometimes a more daring phrase was used, as by al-Ḥallāj, crucified in 922 A.D., who cried out in his ecstasy of communion with God 'I am the Truth'. In some ways he had appeared orthodox, going on pilgrimage to Mecca, and giving up the special mystic's clothing; in other ways he invited objections – he set up a model Ka'bah in his own house, and he said he wanted to die for his beliefs.

The Mystical Orders

Some mystics drew a following of admirers and disciples. A convention of initiation and discipline was often followed, and an organization known as an 'order' (*ṭarīqah*) was often set up. Some of these orders were monastic, living together in monasteries, although the ṣūfīs usually married. Other orders were for wanderers, going from village to village and country to country, and sometimes claiming miracles. They had huge popular appeal; the tombs of 'saints' often became places of pilgrimage. The orders were one of the most influential factors in the spread of Islam into Asia and Africa. Sometimes there was much superstitious practice which offended the orthodox. But an impressive feature was the depth of the devotional life which made the mystics so admired.

The word *ṭarīqah* means 'path', as does the word *sharī'ah*. Thus it may seem that the path of the order is an alternative or rival to the path of the Law. In fact the ṣūfīs were often at pains to justify their mystical path as in no way conflicting with the requirements of the Law. They saw their mystical devotions and practices as additional rather than alternative to what was already laid down for the orthodox.

Al-Ghazālī

One of the most interesting figures in Islamic history is that of al-Ghazālī (died 1111 A.D.). He was brought up with a widely ranging education

41

and became a professor in Baghdad at an early age. Having studied the philosophers in great detail he attacked their views in a famous work entitled *The Inconsistency of the Philosophers* (a famous philosopher in Spain, Ibn Rushd (died 1198 A.D. and called Averroes in Europe) wrote a reply called *The Inconsistency of 'The Inconsistency'*, but failed to re-instate the discipline of philosophy after al-Ghazālī's attack). Another important work of al-Ghazālī was *The Bringing Back to Life of the Sciences of Religion*.

Yet he was not satisfied with the approach of a rationalist theologian any more than with that of the rationalist philosophers. His autobiography describes how, one day, while lecturing, his tongue 'dried up', and he took up the life of a wandering *ṣūfī* in search of peace of mind. He claims to have found this in the experiences of the illumination of the heart in mystical devotion. He rejected the attachment to wealth and position and spent the rest of his life in relative retirement, although he felt bound to share his discoveries with others.

The Shī'īs

So far we have spoken mostly of orthodox Muslims, known as Sunnīs. Even the rationalist philosophers, and most of the mystics regarded themselves as Sunnī. But an important minority in the Muslim world, resident mainly in Persia and parts of Iraq, are known as Shī'īs. This Arabic word means 'sectarian'. Historically the split in the Muslim community went back to the death of the fourth caliph 'Alī, in 661 A.D. He and his followers had rejected the claims of the Umayyad family to take over the caliphate. The Shī'īs believed that 'Alī's sons, first Hasan and then Husayn, should succeed to the caliphate; the first was induced to giving up his claim, but the second was killed in battle at Karbalā in 680 A.D. This 'martyrdom' of Husayn, as Shī'īs regard it, is remembered and re-enacted annually.

The Shī'ī claim that the caliphate should be within the family of the Prophet through the descendants of his son-in-law, 'Alī, is still held. The Sunnī caliphs have never been recognized, and rival *imāms* led the community of the Shī'īs until the twelfth *imām* disappeared in 874 A.D. Shī'īs believe that he and his successors are in hiding, waiting to return to institute a righteous caliphate when the time is ripe. One branch of the Shī'īs believe that it was the seventh *imām* who went into hiding; this group are called Ismā'īlīs after the name of their seventh *imām*, Ismā'īl. The Ismā'īlīs had a chequered history; they were in control of Egypt for a time, and they also organized a state in Northern Persia from which they sent out against their enemies the famous *hashishin* (from which 'assassin'

8. A Shī'ī Mosque, built by Shah Abbas in the 17th century
in Isfahan, Iran

is derived) who would do anything under the hope of regaining the
'Paradise' which their leader had shown them while they were under the
influence of drugs. The subsequent history of this movement is much more
respectable. Their philosophers and poets were often men of great insight.
Their current leader, the Agha Khan, has led this community to great
prosperity, especially in East Africa.

Non-Muslims Under Muslim Rule

We have already seen how early Islam spread without forcing con-
version upon Christians and Jews. Indeed those communities sometimes
welcomed the guaranteed tolerance of other monotheistic religions which
Islam offered. Even in the context of animist tribesmen in North Africa,
and of Hindus in India Muslims showed themselves ready to co-exist with
non-Muslims, provided those non-Muslims were not hostile to Islam.
It is significant that when the Jews were driven out of Christian Spain
they fled for protection to the Muslims of the Ottoman Empire, where
their legal and social rights as Jews could be preserved.

6

SUCCESSES AND DISAPPOINTMENTS
IN ISLAMIC HISTORY

Ideal and Practice

A famous comic history of England classifies all the various rulers as 'a good thing' or 'a bad thing'. There is a similar variety among the individuals and movements of Islamic history. There are in every age the achievements and the disappointments of good Muslims, and there are the times when nominal or heretical Muslims gain the upper hand or are worsted. Through all these ups and downs Muslims believe that their religion has survived, and that it has often saved the situation; and, as we shall see in the last chapter, they also believe that it will continue to inspire them for a better future.

Muslims do not however judge their religion purely on the basis of how past Muslims have lived by it. Very often Islam has been neglected, both at a devotional and at a practical or legal level. In such circumstances it is not fair to blame Islam for social ills which have taken root because of neglect of Islam. Christians or Communists do not want their religion or ideology to be judged on the basis of their followers' abuses and neglect, but on the basis of their ideals and achievements. If one is comparing Islamic history with some other phase of world history, it is important to be fair, and to compare the ideal or best in one tradition with the ideal or best in the other tradition, and to compare worst with worst, failings with failings. If this chapter touches upon some failings in Islamic history, these could easily be paralleled by comparable failings in, for example, Christian history. We learn by others' mistakes, but we also learn by our own. Muslims are often the first to point out that their ancestors or they themselves have not put into practice the high ideals of service to God and service to man which their religion teaches. But Muslims believe that this makes those ideals more and not less urgent.

The Decline of the Caliphate

After the theoretically ideal society of the Rightly-Guided caliphs, and after the universalist achievement of the Umayyads with their empire from India to Spain, we have seen that the 'Abbāsids enjoyed an initial century of political and intellectual prestige. It is true that they no longer controlled Spain, but there was a truly international society as Arab caliphs used Persian administrators, Turkish soldiers and Christian scholars. But certain internal and external points of decay developed.

The efficiency and honesty of the administration and tax-collection was undermined, perhaps by too much luxury at the court, if one accepts the criticisms of some contemporary Muslims. The unity of orthodoxy was being strained by Shī'īs, philosophers and extremist mystics. Still worse, social unrest and then rebellion among slaves challenged the security of the heartlands of the empire, while in many provinces, notably Egypt and Persia, there were growing partisan movements which led to the setting up of independent dynasties. Some of these continued to honour the central office of the caliph, but others, like the Persian dynasty of the Buyids, moved into Baghdad, blinded the caliph and imposed a puppet caliph; they instituted a division between the spiritual authority of the caliph and the actual authority of the Buyid prince or *amir*. One can tell the attitude of these princes when one hears that one of them used to keep savage lions chained at the foot of his throne in order to terrorize anyone who came before him.

After 100 years of virtual rule over Baghdad and much of the surrounding empire, the Buyids were expelled in 1055 A.D. by much more orthodox Turkish rulers, the Saljūqs. They attempted to re-unite the fragmented empire. It was one of their chief ministers, Nizām al-Mulk (died 1092, assassinated by an Ismā'īlī), who gives us one of the most vivid pictures of the society of his day and who tried to prescribe for the recovery of the empire from its decline and sickness.

Nizām al-Mulk

A Muslim biographer describes the relationship of the Grand Vizier Nizām al-Mulk to the Saljūq sultan as follows:

> For 20 years . . . Nizām al-Mulk had all the power concentrated in his own hand, while the sultan had nothing else to do but to sit upon the throne or to enjoy his hunting.

Nizām al-Mulk set up the academy where al-Ghazālī taught, and was also a patron of the famous Persian poet 'Umar Khayyām (died about 1123 A.D.); but his chief fame was as an administrator and as the author of *The Book of Government*. He ensured that the authority of the central government was respected and set up good communications and even a spy system to keep in touch with the provinces. Above all he tried to ensure that justice was practised everywhere. There is in mediaeval political and ethical writing a constant attack upon the injustice that came from neglecting Islam. Both practical and spiritual reform and revival are needed to give all men a fair and just condition for their life.

The Crusades

In 1095 A.D. Pope Urban II launched the first Crusade against the Holy Land with the words, 'God wills it'. It would have been more accurate, perhaps, to say that the merchants and princes of Western Europe willed it in order to extend their Mediterranean trade and in order to win glory in battle. The superstitious peasants and townsmen who joined the armies may have had more pious intentions, but they were surely misled. The Crusades were not launched in the spirit of Christian love of one's neighbour or enemy; they were launched for reasons of greed for wealth and territory, of intolerance towards the Eastern Churches, and of ignorance and arrogance towards Islam.

Christians should never speak of the Crusades or of 'crusading' as if they were noble things. They represent one of the most shameful episodes in the life of the Western Churches; as for the Eastern Christians, they suffered more at the hands of their fellow-Christian Crusaders than they had ever suffered from the Muslims. The Muslims, against whom the Crusaders were theoretically fighting, suffered far less than did the Eastern Christians; but one thing which did very understandably suffer in the Muslim world was the spirit of tolerance. Even so the Crusaders were impressed by the nobility of some of the Muslims, notably that of their greatest leader, Salāh al-Dīn (died 1193 A.D. and known as Saladin in Europe).

On the Christian side one passes over the naive attempts to blow down the walls of Jerusalem with trumpet blasts in 1099 and the horrible massacre when the Crusaders stormed the city a few weeks later; one passes over the slaughter of 2,700 prisoners of war by Richard Coeur de Lion in the Third Crusade (1189-92 A.D.) or the pathetic Children's Crusade (1212 A.D.) when the survivors were sold by Christian merchants into slavery. One comes to a more hopeful phase with St. Francis of Assisi who defied the instructions of the papal legate and went unarmed into the camp of the Muslim Sultan of Egypt in 1219 A.D. The Sultan al-Kāmil received him kindly but listened unresponsively to St. Francis's appeal to prove the superiority of Christianity by St. Francis's walking through fire; the Sultan refused to put God to the test and sent his visitor away with gifts for the poor of Italy. A century later another Christian, Raymond Lull (died 1316 A.D. at the hands of a Muslim mob in Tunis), preached powerfully against the use of arms and appealed to Christians to love their enemy. He was called 'The Fool of Love'.

The Mongol Invasion

The Crusades are chiefly important for the local history of the Holy Land and for the indirect effects which they exerted farther afield. There were the good effects of exchange of scientific, technical, agricultural and cultural knowledge, but there was the very bad effect of a hardening of attitudes between Christians and Muslims. The Western Christians often brought back from the Crusades the same sort of caricatures and prejudices of Islam that they had taken with them. The Muslims received a disastrous impression of Christians. But neither Muslims nor Christians suffered as much from each other as they did from a third party – the Mongols.

The nomadic movements and invasions of the Mongol hordes were sensed as a distant threat by both Christians and Muslims from the beginning of the thirteenth century A.D. The Christians, however, hoped that the Mongols might become Christian and help them against the Muslims; but when the Mongols asked for 1,000 Christian missionaries only two went. The Muslim caliph al-Nāṣir (died 1225 A.D.) also hoped to win Mongol support; he was not so much worried by the Crusaders, who never penetrated deep into the Muslim empire, but he was hoping that the Mongols would suppress for him some troublesome rebels in his Northern provinces. The Mongol Chingīz Khān (died about 1227 A.D.) was only too glad to go wherever plunder could be had; but he had no intention of stopping where the caliph asked him to stop. He and his successors pressed on, destroying everything in their path, until Baghdad itself, and with it the 'Abbāsid caliphate, fell in 1258 A.D.

Not long after, the Mongols decided to adopt Islam, and, as fanatical new converts, they tried to force Eastern Christians to follow their example; many of those Christians who refused were massacred. Not only were the material achievements of the 'Abbāsid caliphate destroyed by the Mongols, but so was the international and inter-religious community which had been built up. The Muslim world in the Middle East became and remained more fragmented than ever; there was no figurehead of caliph, and economic, social and political anarchy was such that no sultan either could retrieve the situation. The focus of Islamic achievement shifts away from the Middle East to new empires based on Turkey, Persia and India.

The Mediaeval Empires of Islam

The Ottoman Empire had its origins at the beginning of the fourteenth century A.D. in Anatolia; it spread quickly eastwards as far as Syria and westwards to the Danube. After the decisive defeat of the Crusaders at the Battle of Nicopolis in 1396 A.D., the Ottoman expansion into Europe became still easier, although it was not until 1453 that Byzantium was captured and the great Christian basilica of Santa Sophia was turned into a mosque. By 1529 A.D. the Ottomans had reached the gates of Vienna, and once again Western Europe was stirred into great hostility towards their Muslim neighbours; we have evidence of this in some of Luther's bitter attacks upon Islam, where he uses comparisons between Islam and Rome implying that ritual and politics have deluded both.

It was not these verbal attacks which weakened the Ottoman Empire. Internal decay in terms of corrupt administration and decadent court life were symptoms of the frustration of a military empire which had no more territories into which it could expand and which was finding its existing territories in Europe and Asia unmanageable. There was shortage of money after the influx of silver from America devalued Ottoman currency, yet soldiers now had to be paid in cash rather than with conquered lands. There was food shortage in the neglected and exploited countryside, and there were new problems in the cities as people flooded into them from the country. Slowly but surely the Ottoman Empire became the 'Sick Man of Europe' and finally collapsed in the 1914–1918 World War.

One reason why the Ottomans could not find any outlet to the East was that at the end of the fourteenth century the world conqueror Tīmūr (died 1404 A.D.) set up a great although short-lived empire; he is memorable chiefly for his ruthlessness, but also for the beautiful architecture which he commissioned. After his empire had broken up into petty kingdoms, Persia was again re-united in the sixteenth century by the Ṣafawid Shāhs. They made Shī'ī belief the official faith of Persia, thereby avoiding any possible co-operation with the Sunnī Ottomans. The Ṣafawids are also notable for their patronage of literature and architecture; their capital at Isfahan became one of the world's most beautiful cities, and Western travellers were amazed at it.

48

9. Iran: Front of the Shaykh Lutfullah Mosque in Isfahan, one of the masterpieces of Iranian architecture

10. A view of the Taj Mahal, Agra, India

Further East, in India, Islam was increasing in political strength, especially in the North. The various dynasties of the Delhi Sultanate from the twelfth to the fifteenth century A.D. paved the way for the great Mughal Empire which extended Muslim political control over almost all the subcontinent before the counter-offensive of certain Hindu rulers and the eventual 'take-over' by the East India Company and the British Rāj in the eighteenth and nineteenth centuries A.D. The Mughals used some of the wealth which they amassed during their conquests to build magnificent mosques, palaces and tombs, the most famous of which is the Tāj Mahāl, the tomb built for his wife by the Emperor Shāh Jahān (died 1658 A.D.).

The Expansion of Islam into Africa and South East Asia

Almost unnoticed by the courts of the great mediaeval Muslim empires there was a quiet but steady spread of Islam still further. In India itself it had been the efforts of pious Muslim merchants and the preaching of *sūfi* saints which had led to the greatest numerical gains of converts to Islam; they were more effective than armies in leading people to a voluntary decision to adopt the simple faith in the One God, the impressive discipline of the prayer rite, and membership in a community which knew no caste or colour distinction.

Similarly, from the seventh century A.D. onwards, it is claimed, individual Muslim traders had reached as far as modern Malaysia and Indonesia, and a great wave of conversions to Islam had taken place between the thirteenth and sixteenth centuries. Various conventions in terms of democratic decision-taking and favoured status for women were preserved from previous customary law. Mysticism was again an important movement.

In Africa, again without political pressures or military intervention from the main Muslim empires, Islam also spread. Traders came from North Africa, following both East and West coasts of Africa, following the Nile and traversing the Sahara. They made converts among some of the African rulers who thus established a chain of Muslim kingdoms across Africa south of the Sahara; one of the earliest kings to be converted was in Kanem (near Lake Chad) in about 1090 A.D. Islam did not become a religion of the common people in Africa until comparatively recently, and today it is spreading, in parts rapidly.

11. Mosques and Holy Places are especially crowded during the Month of Rama-
dan; there is usually a special section for women as here in Turkey

7

MODERN MUSLIMS' HOPES FOR THE FUTURE

Memories of Past Glories

Modern Muslims have often lived in situations of disappointment. They have frequently suffered more than they have gained by the way in which Western colonialism and imperialism spread over the Middle East, Asia and Africa. The collapse of the political prestige of the Muslim empires brought a sense of defeat. So did the abolition of the office of the caliphate in 1924 A.D. after it had been revived for the last 150 years by the Ottomans in an attempt to draw the Islamic world together again. Muslims asked themselves why Western society had made such rapid strides, while society in the Muslim world seemed to stagnate. They could not blame Islam itself for this stagnation, for they remembered how Islam in the past had acted as a focal point for the establishment of a mighty and humane civilization; they thought of the pious simplicity of the Prophet and his 'Companions'; they thought of the 'Golden Age' of the 'Abbāsid caliphate with its cultural achievements; they thought of the more recent military and political prestige of the Ottoman and Mughal Empires. They asked themselves what had gone wrong.

It was easy to blame the West for the many commercial and diplomatic abuses which the Muslim countries were suffering in the nineteenth and twentieth centuries A.D. But there were some more self-critical Muslims who realized that there must also be internal reasons for the decline of Islamic society, and for its apparent inability to recover. Three basic schools of thought stand out. There were – and are – the traditionalists, the modernists and the secularists. They preach revival, reformation or revolution. We shall try to look fairly and sensitively at each in turn.

12. In the shade of the arcades surrounding Al-Azhar's great courtyard in Cairo, a Muslim, leaning against an ancient column, sits studying

The Traditionalists

We have just seen that many Muslims have wondered why Islam, with its glorious past, should have encountered such difficulties and disappointments in the modern world. Already under the declining Ottomans there was the attempt to revive the caliphate, but local nationalisms in the Balkans and in the Arab world were too deeply rooted. Indian Muslims supported the idea of the caliphate, partly for anti-British political reasons (even welcoming the support of Gandhi), but also for spiritual reasons. The new patterns of Western law offended many Muslims, especially when they threatened to interfere with the Law, *shari'ah* (although this fear was more imagined than real). They dreamed of a Muslim government once more so that the neglected and violated principles of Islam could be re-introduced and enforced.

An important movement in the last years of the nineteenth century, and an aspiration which exists to the present day among many Muslims, is that of Pan-Islam. The idea of an international Islamic government, or at least confederation, is partly a defensive alliance against the Western powers and, more recently, the Communist world. But there is also the more positive aspect that the supporters of Pan-Islam believe that the secret for success in the modern world lies in recovering the moral values, the social legislation and the political unity which were there in classical Islamic history.

One of the greatest exponents of this Pan-Islam was Jamāl al-Dīn Afghānī (died 1897 A.D.). He travelled all over the Muslim world, from Afghanistan to India, from Arabia to Egypt and Turkey, back to India and Egypt, and then to London, Paris and St. Petersburg, before returning to Persia and Turkey (where he died under virtual house arrest because the Ottoman sultan feared his influence). He called the Western nations 'the greedy ones', and he also criticized any narrow and selfish nationalism among Ottomans, Persians or Egyptians, if this hindered the eventual cause of international Islam. He was sufficiently realistic to see that at that time a local nationalism was often necessary to throw off colonialist power or local autocracy.

One of the most influential recent movements of this kind has been that of the 'Muslim Brotherhood'. Since being suppressed by President Nasser in Egypt, they have gone underground there, although they re-emerged for a while during the presidency of the late Anwar Sadat whose assassination was claimed by another extremist and fundamentalist Islamic group. Other Islamic countries, notably Syria, are feeling the sometimes violent challenge of the 'Brothers' who aspire to political and legal authority for an Islamic state.

13. Muslims offering prayers in Badshahi Mosque at Lahore

The idea of an Islamic state has been realized in only a few countries. Saudi Arabia claims to regulate its society according to the strictest Ḥanbalī legal school. Morocco is ruled by a monarchy and political party which lay great emphasis on their faithfulness to Islamic ideals and models. Pakistan is perhaps the most interesting example of a modern state which has been founded with the self-conscious aim to conduct all its affairs in accordance with Islamic precedent; this is especially true since the Islamization advocated by the late founder of the Jama'at Islami, Mawlānā Mawdūdī, has been applied by the military government which took control in the late 1970s.

Pakistan was founded in 1947 from those North-Western and North-Eastern parts of the sub-continent of India which had the densest population of Muslims. The aspiration for a separate Islamic state was built partly on frustration with trying to preserve their Islamic identity in face of the previously British government, and partly on fear that the Hindu majority would swamp the Muslim minority (even though it was a minority of about 100 million). The separate state was proclaimed and yet there have been repeated difficulties and disappointments in trying to achieve a satisfactory Islamic constitution. Economic pressures, political corruption, inability to establish good relations with India, and ideological threats from extremists (fanatical Muslims and fanatical Communists) have all combined to make it difficult for the young state.

One of the father figures of Pakistan, the poet Iqbal, once wrote 'Politics dethroned religion'; he was writing of the way that a local nationalism could be a danger if it was an end in itself, whereas it should be harnessed to the setting up of an international brotherhood. Many Pakistanis have held on to Iqbal's dream of their country being dedicated to the establishment of moral and spiritual values for the benefit of all mankind, and to the glory of God. Pakistan has been the headquarters of the World Muslim Congress, while Saudi Arabia has sponsored the perhaps more political World Muslim League as well as welcomed the headquarters in Jiddah of the Organization of the Islamic Conference of Muslim heads of state.

Most dramatic and sudden among traditionalist reactions has been the overthrow of the Iranian monarchy by a popular revolution led mainly by Shi'i clergy. Ayatollah Khomeini returned to Iran in 1979 after a long exile in Iraq and France from where he had rightly attacked the economic and political dependence of Iran upon the West.

In this he had the sometimes unacknowledged support of more secular and often socialist-oriented 'revolutionaries' but the Islamic regime that was immediately established turned violently against such secularists (and against minority groups like Bahá'ís who are seen as heretics for allowing another prophet, the nineteenth century Bahá'alláh, after Muhammad). There has been a wave of terror in terms of torture and executions which has exceeded even that of the late Shah's secret police. After the initial attraction of a bloodless revolution in the name of Islam, the subsequent denial of human rights and the economic stagnation and decline of the country have given many Muslims second thoughts about giving such judicial and governmental power to the clergy, however important it may be to have their moral and spiritual guidance.

The Modernists

We have illustrated the variety among the traditionalists in the Muslim world in recent times; some were concerned with structures and the letter of the law; others had dreams of spiritual revival leading to univer-

14. One of the science laboratories at Al-Azhar where students come together from many lands

sal peace. Among the modernists too one may take examples of some who would have so reformed the structures of Islam that the orthodox protested that this was the dreaded 'innovation'; on the other hand there were some unmistakably orthodox Muslim leaders who brought real reforms by breathing a truer spirit into old structures.

Sir Sayyid Ahmad Khan in the late nineteenth century in India is an example of one who stressed that Islam could be compatible with the modern world if Muslim structures were changed. As a first step Muslims were to be better educated. He set up the famous Anglo-Muhammadan College at Aligarh in North India, and here he prepared many Muslims for eventual positions of authority and responsibility. He supported Islam by rational and 'natural' arguments, and therefore he was criticized by the conservatives for compromising the authority of revelation. He defended himself by saying that the Author of nature was the Author of revelation so that there could be no clash. He criticized the theologians and jurists of Islam for those interpretations of Islam which appeared to clash with the modern world.

Another critic of traditionalism who died in 1905 A.D., seven years later

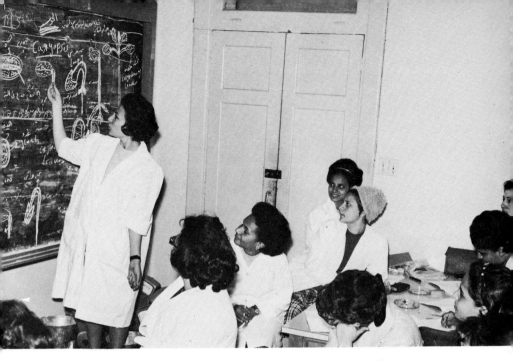

15. Women at Al-Azhar have proved that science can co-exist with ancient customs and beliefs. Here they are seen attending a lecture

than Sir Sayyid Ahmad Khan, was the Egyptian Muhammad 'Abdūh. He too made an educational institution his base of operations, the famous al-Azhar University in Cairo. Muslims come to al-Azhar from all over the world, and its influence and that of its teachers is thus enormous. Muhammad 'Abdūh criticized traditionalism as 'being bound by the past' (*taqlid*). He was equally critical of those who were carried away by everything modern and Western, and in this connection he criticized Sir Sayyid Ahmad Khan. He did not see a ready made answer in the past, nor in the modern world. He believed that Judaism was too exclusivist and authoritarian to reform the world, and that Christianity was too sentimental with its love of neighbours and too world-denying and ascetic, judging from the church as he saw it. Islam on the other hand he saw as suited to the reform of the world with what he claimed as its rational, practical and inter-racial characteristics.

Although Muhammad 'Abdūh recognized that many abuses had crept into Islamic history because men had slavishly followed the rulings of past Muslim leaders, this did not deter him from seeking human solutions. Divine revelation must be understood and re-interpreted in

59

each age, and those suitably trained must exercise the responsibility of taking decisions for themselves. He spoke of 're-opening the gates of individual decision (*ijtihād*)' which had been practically closed since the mediaeval jurists had decreed that all Muslims were bound to follow the precepts of the various law schools. In any modernist re-interpretation he was not trying to 'turn a Muslim into a modern man', but he was trying to 'show that a modern man can be Muslim'. Muhammad 'Abdūh's viewpoint has remained widely influential to the present day.

Recent leaders of Egypt, like President Nasser and President Sadat, took pains to justify their economic and political reforms and initiatives both at home and abroad in terms of loyalty to broad Islamic ideals of brotherhood, responsibility, peace-making etc. Similar trends in Bangladesh, independent from Pakistan since 1973, have regularly been interpreted in terms of Islamic principles; the same is true of countries like Algeria which emerged from its long struggle for independence from France with a strong modernist, rationalist and socialist vision but with a determination to regulate this in terms of Islamic criteria. Many Muslims, from N. Africa, the Indian sub-continent and the Middle East (including Turkey), who now live in the West as new settlers or migrant workers, welcome modern patterns of education, economics and social structures on condition that they are checked and disciplined by Islamic principles.

The Secularists

This group of secularists includes at one extreme those who still regard themselves as Muslims, but who argue that political, educational and legal matters should not be entrusted to the religious leaders. At the other extreme it includes those who adopt an anti-religious ideology, attacking not only the religious leadership but the whole phenomenon of belief in God.

The most striking example of a secularizing revolution in the modern Muslim world is Turkey in the 1920s. Under the leadership of Kemal Ataturk all religious authority, legal, educational and financial, was abolished. Traditional Muslim dress, including the fez for men and the veil for women, was forbidden. The teaching of Arabic, and all other theological education were stopped. Yet Ataturk himself said: 'If religion exists, then I cannot destroy it'. It is significant that in the last thirty years religious education has been brought back, religious issues have been very important in recent elections, mosque attendance has risen, and Turkish pilgrims are as numerous as those from many other countries on pilgrimage to Mecca.

16. A late 19th century mosque in the heart of Cairo

17. A street scene in an old part of Cairo

In Soviet Asia and Afghanistan Muslims have faced severer persecution, but the Communist secularism which has opposed them has not been part of their own culture. In the modern Middle East, in pre- and post-independence Bangladesh and periodically in Indonesia, there has been a new type of social and political protest initiated by Muslims themselves. Arab socialism, for example, may often appear as much the enemy of Islamic traditionalism as it is of neo-colonialism and capitalism. But part of the zeal behind the search for socialism is the properly Islamic zeal for a just society and for peace and brotherhood. Islamic revival and reform have sometimes been preached by Muslim governments whose corruption and exploitation made their religious claims lose credibility. Yet religious loyal-ties are deeply held by most Muslims and it is a significant fact that social-ism, and even communism, are being preached in many parts of the modern Muslim world without the usual appeal for atheism, or for class-struggle (rejected by Islam with its doctrine of brotherhood and its conviction that God apportions man's material condition).

Among young people in the modern Muslim world there is questioning of political structures and there is frequent student unrest; there is some-times tension over traditional family loyalties and duties, especially as films and television show new patterns of romance and different cultural values. Especially in the towns and in the Arab world there may be a lack of discipline over regular observance of the prayer. But it is still rare to find an atheistic Muslim who will declare that he is not a Muslim and who will attack Islam.

Two places where there have been particular visions of a 'secular' state have been Palestine and Lebanon. The Muslim and Christian Arabs who refused to negotiate the United Nations proposal in 1948 for the partition of Palestine into two states of Israel and Palestine held up a vision of a single Palestinian state with equal citizenship for Jews, Christians and Muslims. The events of the last thirty years and more have led some of them to entertain the establishment of a smaller, independent Palestine alongside an Israel which would have withdrawn from territories occupied in war; the new Palestine would ensure equality for all.

Lebanon bears much of the brunt of the Palestine conflict but has also lived through many years of virtually civil war; it is constitutionally an inter-religious state with careful and even jealous division of power between the equally balanced Christian and Muslim groups. Some Lebanese now believe that the only way to maintain the unity of the country would be to declare it a secular state. They want to keep religion out of politics, so that economic and political conflicts are not inflamed by religious passions.

Future Prospects for Islam

Western observers who judged Islam on the basis of Muslims' failures rather than their achievements used to predict the imminent collapse of Islam. Today there is plenty of evidence that Islam is a vital force. It is still taught and observed by a world-wide community. International and local Islamic organizations keep alive the hope that Muslims may together make a contribution to world stability, prosperity and moral values. The inter-racial dimension of Islam has encouraged its expansion in Africa, and, with a certain self-contradiction, in the Black Islam of North America. Islam has survived the revolutions of Turkey and the Communist world, and Islam has shown that it has much to contribute in lending a moral and spiritual dynamic to the social reforms and revolutions in many parts of the Muslim world.

In relationship with other religious traditions, notably with Christianity (with which it has been so involved down the centuries), there are signs of a greater readiness for mutual understanding. In places like Lebanon the very existence of the country depends on a partnership between Muslim and Christian. In many African situations Muslims and Christians are co-operating in building new nations. In Asia Christian minorities may try to contribute to the development of a predominantly Muslim society; in many European countries and in Britain Muslim minorities are making their contribution to economic and social stability.

It is increasingly important that Muslims and Christians should learn to live together, to serve each other's interests, and so to serve God better. One cannot be blind to the theological and social differences and tensions, but there can be much more to unite us than to divide us. Muslims have much to share with Christians. They have much to share with the world beyond. In all of this they believe that God will always guide them, and support them, and judge them.